Pebble™ Plus

Keeping Healthy

Taking Care of My Teeth

by Terri DeGezelle

Consulting Editor: Gail Saunders-Smith, PhD

Consultant: Amy Grimm, MPH
Program Director, National Center for Health Education
New York, New York

Capstone

Mankato, Minnesota

Pebble Plus is published by Capstone Press.
151 Good Counsel Drive, P.O. Box 669, Mankato, Minnesota 56002.
www.capstonepress.com

1 2 3 4 5 6 10 09 08 07 06 05

Library of Congress Cataloging-in-Publication Data
DeGezelle, Terri, 1955–
   Taking care of my teeth / by Terri DeGezelle.
   p.cm.—(Pebble plus. Keeping healthy.)
   Summary: "Simple text and photographs present ways to take care of your teeth."—Provided by publisher.
   Includes bibliographical references and index.
   ISBN 0-7368-4264-0 (hardcover)
   1. Teeth—Care and hygiene—Juvenile literature. I. Title. II. Series.
RK63.D44 2006
617.6'01—dc22
                                       2004026750

Editorial Credits
Sarah L. Schuette, editor; Jennifer Bergstrom, designer; Stacy Foster, photo resource coordinator

Photo Credits
Capstone Press/Karon Dubke, all

The author dedicates this book to Gabrielle and Nathaniel Willaert.

Note to Parents and Teachers

The Keeping Healthy set supports science standards related to physical health and life skills for personal health. This book describes and illustrates how to take care of your teeth. The images support early readers in understanding the text. The repetition of words and phrases helps early readers learn new words. This book also introduces early readers to subject-specific vocabulary words, which are defined in the Glossary section. Early readers may need assistance to read some words and to use the Table of Contents, Glossary, Read More, Internet Sites, and Index sections of the book.

Table of Contents

My Amazing Teeth

I have 20 baby teeth
in my mouth.
My baby teeth will fall out
as I grow.

Then permanent teeth grow.

I will have 32 teeth

when I am an adult.

The top part of my tooth

is the crown.

Teeth grow out of my gums.

Roots hold teeth inside

my mouth.

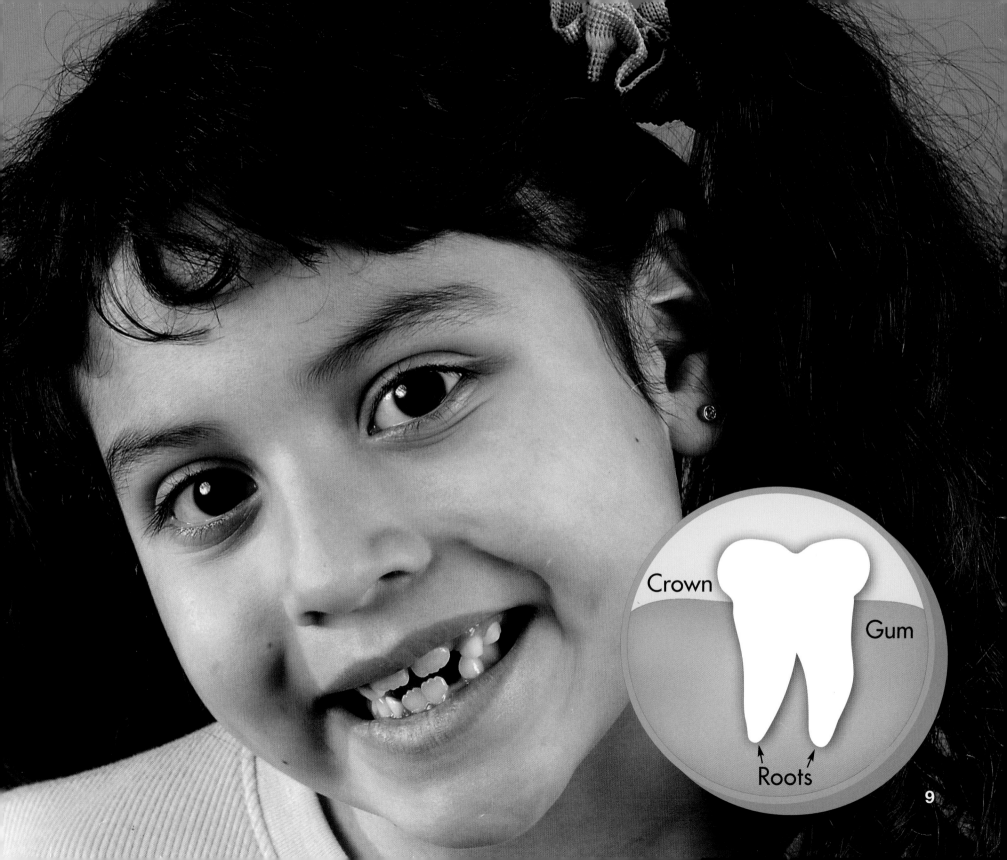

Crown

Gum

Roots

Front teeth cut
and tear food.
Back teeth grind
and crush food.

The Dentist's Office

I go to the dentist's office
twice a year.

I get my teeth cleaned.

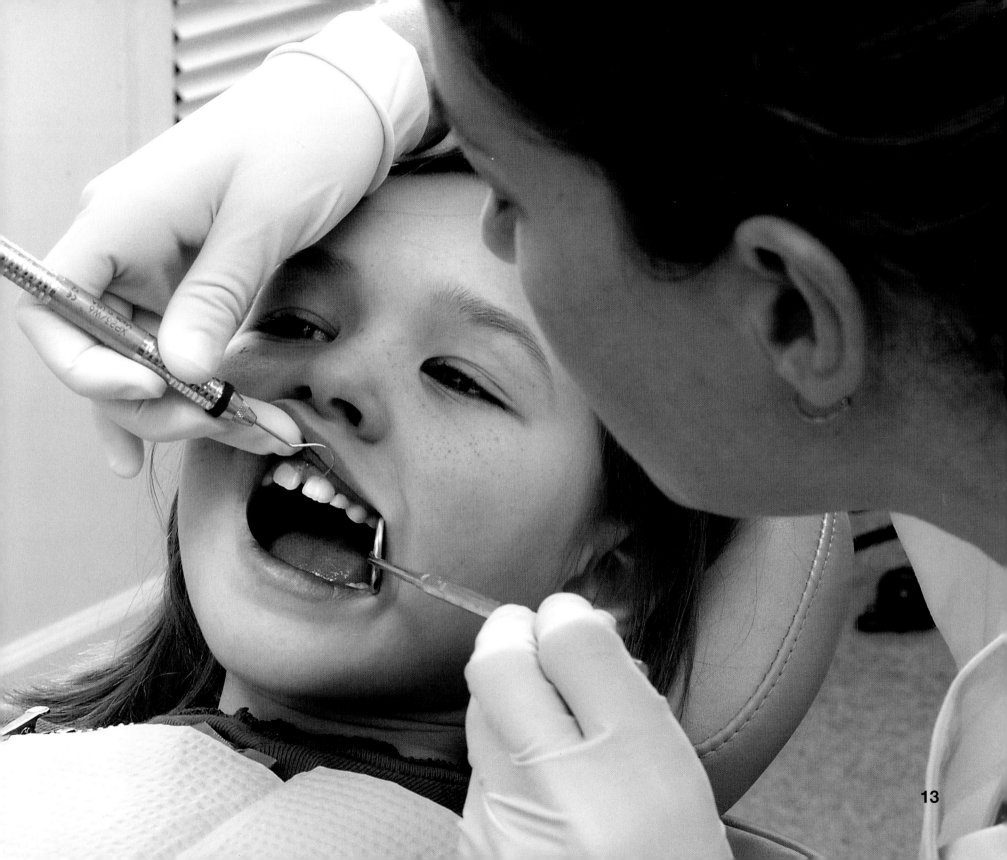

The dentist looks

at x-rays of my teeth.

He checks for cavities.

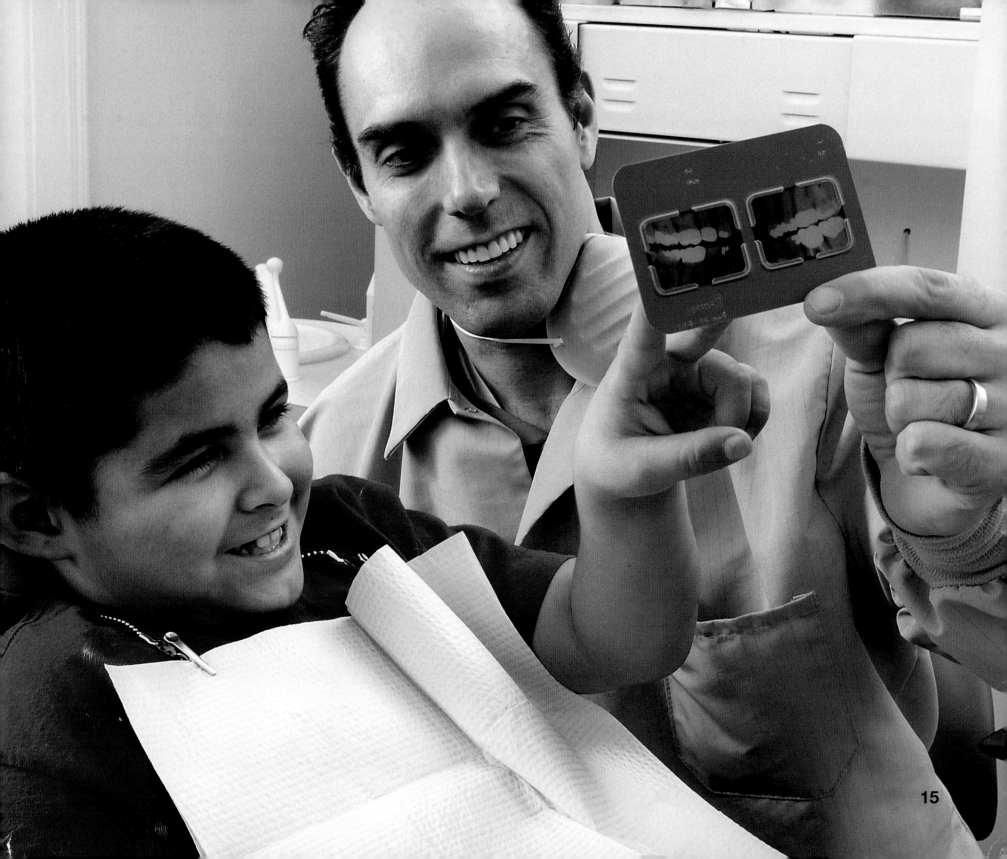

Healthy Teeth

I brush my teeth every day.

I brush in the morning,

after meals, and at night.

I floss between my teeth
every day.

I keep my mouth healthy
when I take care of
my teeth.

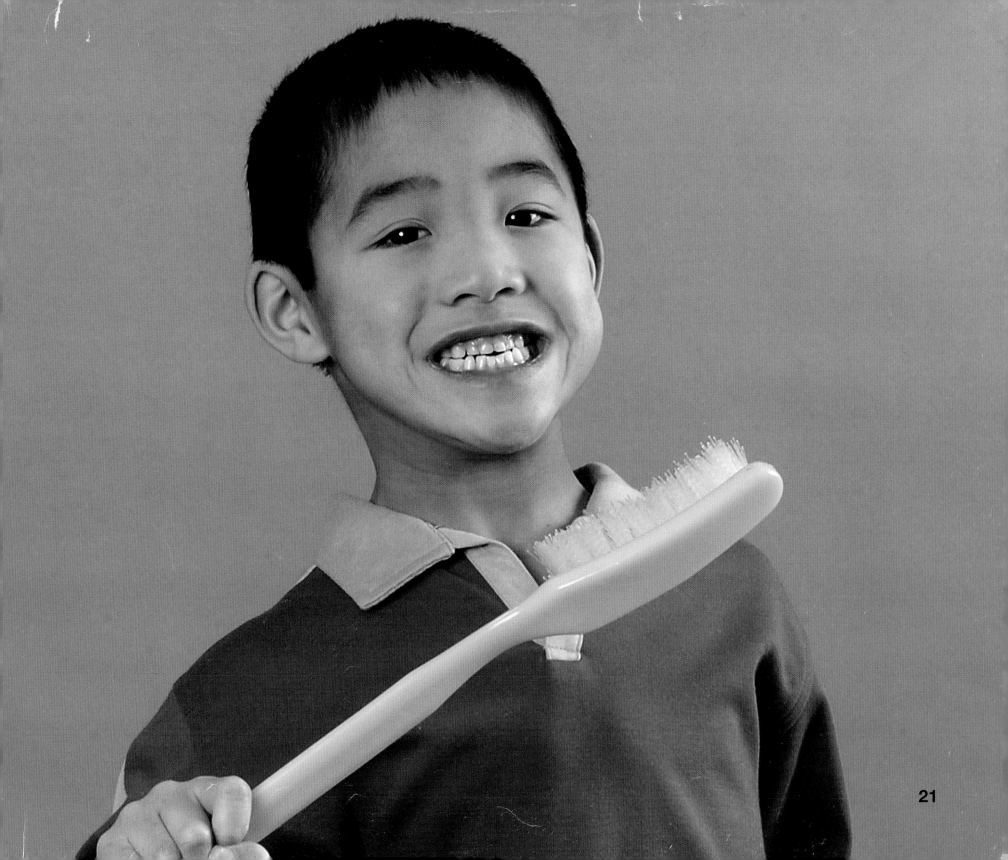

Glossary

cavity—a decayed or broken-down part of a tooth

crown—the top part of the tooth that you can see

dentist—a person who is trained to examine, clean, and fix problems with teeth

floss—to put a thin piece of dental floss between your teeth to help keep your teeth clean

gum—the firm, pink skin around the base of the tooth

root—the part of the tooth that holds it in the mouth

x-ray—a picture of the inside of a tooth

Read More

Curry, Don L. *Take Care of Your Teeth.* Rookie Read-About Health. New York: Children's Press, 2005.

Salzmann, Mary Elizabeth. *Taking Care of Your Teeth.* Healthy Habits. Edina, Minn.: Abdo, 2004.

Vogel, Elizabeth. *Brushing My Teeth.* Clean and Healthy All Day Long. New York: PowerKids Press, 2001.

Internet Sites

FactHound offers a safe, fun way to find Internet sites related to this book. All of the sites on FactHound have been researched by our staff.

Here's how:

1. Visit *www.facthound.com*

2. Type in this special code **0736842640** for age-appropriate sites. Or enter a search word related to this book for a more general search.

3. Click on the **Fetch It** button.

FactHound will fetch the best sites for you!

Index

Word Count: 125
Grade: 1
Early-Intervention Level: 16